KU-310-232

Liberating
the Letter

A proposal to privatise the Post Office

IAN SENIOR

Published by
THE INSTITUTE OF ECONOMIC AFFAIRS
1983

First published July 1983

© THE INSTITUTE OF ECONOMIC AFFAIRS 1983

ISSN 0073-9103
ISBN 0-255 36164-5

Printed in Great Britain by
Goron Pro-Print Ltd., Churchill Industrial Estate, Lancing, Sussex
Set in Univers 9 on 11pt Series 689

Contents

Preface

IEA *Research Monographs* accommodate texts in which the emphasis is normally on the empirical content derived from documentary evidence, field studies, or other sources.

The author of *Research Monograph* 38, Mr Ian Senior, has for many years maintained a close interest in the Post Office since beginning his working career with four and a half years at Post Office headquarters in the 1960s when it was a government department. In 1970, shortly after the Post Office became a public corporation, the IEA published a study by him entitled *The Postal Service: Competition or Monopoly?*,[1] in which he argued for the removal of the Post Office statutory letter monopoly and a reconsideration of standard nationwide charges irrespective of differential costs. Critical of the Post Office's poor record on labour productivity and of its practice of cross-subsidising other parts of its business from monopoly profits earned by the letter service, he called for restrictions on private competition in the postal market to be lifted as a spur to the Post Office in raising efficiency for the benefit of its tens of millions of users.

Thirteen years later, Mr Senior's views have moved on with the times and with technological developments. Though the Post Office retains its statutory monopoly, he no longer regards its removal—desirable though that remains—as the key issue of policy. The very survival of the Post Office in the face of the dawning electronic revolution is at stake. The 'crutch of an archaic and near-obsolete monopoly' has ceased to guarantee the Post Office a future. On the contrary, it has become a dangerous brake on its capacity for acquiring the commercial skills it will require to stay in business in the new competitive age creeping up on it.

Mr Senior authoritatively describes how the electronic revolution will change the services provided by the Post Office beyond recognition over the coming decade—both its mail service, which consists of carrying physical objects, and its counter service,

---

[1] IEA Background Memorandum 3.

which is concerned with money transactions. Letters written on paper will increasingly be replaced by the 'electronic letter', while the Post Office's paper-based banking, money transfer and agency services will be transformed by automated teller machines, point-of-sale registers, home banking, and a variety of electronic systems for transferring funds based on plastic cards. Thus the challenge of private competition is on the horizon for the Post Office whether or not it retains a monopoly of the paper letter. That monopoly will ultimately become irrelevant because it will have no exclusive rights over the electronic letter. If the Post Office is to compete in the new high-technology communications industry of tomorrow, it must learn to compete freely today in a traditional industry where government privileges have hitherto given it a head-start.

It is for this reason that, in *Research Monograph* 38, Mr Senior argues powerfully for the immediate removal of the Post Office's letter monopoly—as well as because it would help promote a better service for users during the transition to electronic mail. Painstakingly, he documents the performance record of the Post Office which, though good (or less bad) by the standards of other countries' statutory monopolies, reveals a decline in the quality of its postal service (in terms of speed and reliability of delivery) and such uneconomic practices as cross-subsidisation of different activities, uniform nationwide pay-scales, and pay-rates in excess of what the labour market required. Not the least cause for criticism is inadequate innovation, with the counter services in grave danger of becoming technologically obsolete after enjoying for many years a *de facto* monopoly over a wide range of government agency services (Mr Senior reminds us that counter clerks use the backs of envelopes for computations as though electronic calculators did not exist). With incisive analysis he punctures the hoary old myths—perpetuated not least by the Post Office itself to justify the retention of its monopoly—that the post is a 'social service' and that rural mail is inherently unprofit-able. He offers convincing reasons for supposing that country areas would continue to be served in a régime of competition without uniform nationwide tariffs. He marshals an impressive array of evidence—such as the continual and determined efforts by profit-conscious entrepreneurs to find loopholes in the law to compete with the Post Office, private initiatives during the 1971 postal strike, and the expansion of courier services in the past decade—to demonstrate that there is a large volume of private resources available and keen to serve the postal market if permitted.

For Mr Senior, the removal of the letter monopoly is now merely a first, if essential and urgent, step to enable the Post Office to stand a chance of surviving the electronic revolution. More radical changes are urgently required if its management is to have the incentive and flexibility to innovate to meet the emerging competition successfully. He argues that nothing short of privatisation of the Post Office will provide that incentive and flexibility. Moreover, the time is now ripe. The Post Office is currently profitable and has good prospects of remaining so without the letter monopoly if it can efficiently harness its advantages of a national network, specialised equipment, trained staff, and experience accumulated over a century or more. There is every reason to believe that the public would take up the offer of shares in it.

Mr Senior further proposes the separation of the mail from the counter services before they are offered for sale to the public as two distinct companies—which he suggests might be called Post Office plc and Counter Services plc respectively. Just as the telecommunications side of the old Post Office was hived off from the existing business because they were two heterogeneous operations, the same logic applies with equal force to splitting the mail and counter services. Although the electronic revolution will profoundly affect both services, each will be affected so differently that, in order to cope with it, they must have the freedom to develop independently. It will also be essential to exclude the possibility of cross-subsidisation between the two.

Mr Senior believes that, in the light of recent successful management buy-outs, there is good reason to hope that Post Office executives would welcome the opportunity to buy shares in Post Office plc and Counter Services plc in order to enjoy some of the profits and capital values created by their efforts. They should also welcome the managerial freedom which privatisation would bring to set economic tariffs, pursue only profitable activities, and re-invest profits as and where they (rather than government) saw fit. However, he anticipates the resistance of postmen and counter clerks who, though they may find some attraction in being offered shares at a discount, have long cherished the Post Office's letter monopoly. Reminding them that their jobs are already at risk from the new technologies and that the letter monopoly cannot afford them protection for much longer, he poses a devastating question which they and their trade union representatives must think about very seriously: Do you have a better chance of maintaining your jobs in the new competitive world if you begin to work for a privatised concern *now* or if you cling to one with an outmoded historical status until it is too late?

The reader will arrive at the end of this penetrating analysis of the Post Office past, present and future struck by an inexplicable paradox which the author highlights in the opening pages, namely, when the air is thick with talk of privatisation and the Post Office is such an obvious candidate, why is it never mentioned? In view of the powerful case mounted by Ian Senior, it is to be hoped that any government in the 1980s will place this state-owned enterprise somewhere near the top of its list of privatisation prospects.

Although the constitution of the Institute requires it to dissociate its Trustees, Directors and Advisers from the author's arguments and conclusions, it offers this *Research Monograph* as an important initiative to open up debate about the future of an institution whose activities touch the life of everyone in this country but have for too long been immune from thoroughgoing objective dissection.

June 1983   Martin Wassell

The Author

IAN SENIOR was born in 1938 and educated at Sedbergh School and Trinity College, Oxford, where he was a scholar in modern languages. Later he took an MSc(Econ.) at University College, London. His career began with four and a half years at Post Office headquarters where he was latterly private secretary to the Junior Minister. Following two years at Liberal Party headquarters, he became a business consultant and is now a director of an economic consultancy.

Mr Senior's previous contributions to the IEA have been *The Postal Service—Competition or Monopoly?* (Background Memorandum 3, 1970) and a commentary in *Bureaucracy: Servant or Master?* (Hobart Paperback 5, 1973).

Acknowledgements

The author wishes to thank Alison Stevens for her research assistance, and the Post Office for supplying data and background information.

I.S.

The IEA gratefully acknowledges the assistance of The Scottish Centre of Political Economy towards the cost of this *Research Monograph.*

ONE

Introduction

Some activities have been undertaken by the state for so long that most people are unaware they were once private. The postal service is one such activity. Where the correct boundary lies between government activity and commercial enterprise is rightly a matter for discussion. Most would concede that government employees are best at administering the edicts of their political masters whilst entrepreneurs are best at providing the goods and services that are demanded in the market. The current debate on the merits of privatisation should therefore be viewed not as an ideological conflict between left and right, but rather as a search for ways of permitting both groups of people—state employees and entrepreneurs—to do what they are best at.

A surprising feature of the current debate about which state-owned activities should be privatised is that the postal service is never mentioned. Yet its former partner in the Post Office, the telecommunications service, is frequently put at the top of the list. Perhaps the main reason is that for many years the postal service has been thought of as a loss-maker, in contrast to the rapidly expanding and profitable telecommunications system. But this is far from true, since the postal service has made a profit in each of the past six years and is set to make a further substantial profit in 1982-83.

The first Thatcher Government declared its intention to privatise a number of major concerns such as British Airways and British Leyland as soon as they were profitable. The postal service is such an obvious candidate that it is difficult to understand why it has been overlooked for so long. In this *Research Monograph*, I shall argue that privatising the Post Office is in the interests not only of the users of its services but also of those who work for it.

TWO

The Post Office's Record

Criticism of the mail service

It is commonplace to criticise the performance of the Post Office, in particular the mail service.[1] The counter service and the National Girobank generally attract fewer public complaints. This may be because the Girobank competes with the high-street banks, and the counter service is largely in private hands with 20,832 scale payment sub-offices in 1982 compared with 1,573 crown offices.[2] It is true that most sub-offices enjoy a local monopoly of the services they provide since it is Post Office policy to limit their number by requiring a distance between them of one mile in towns and two miles in rural areas. Nevertheless, most sub-post-masters gain a significant part of their income from non-Post Office work in competition with other shops. They are therefore likely to be motivated by a wish to satisfy their customers.

Although the mail service bears the brunt of criticism, some of it is probably unjustified. The often used excuse that something has been 'delayed' in the post when in reality it has not yet been sent exemplifies the truism that *les absents ont toujours tort*. The quality of the postal service *has* deteriorated in certain respects;[3] but so have many privately provided services in recent years. Most people have a story about how impossible it is to find a plumber to replace a washer. So the point at issue is not that postal services have got worse compared with a generation ago. Nor is it that Post Office tariffs have risen more rapidly than the retail price index in the past decade. The question is whether services or prices or both would be keener if the post were run privately under competitive conditions.

---

[1] In 1981-82, 73 per cent of 'representations' received by the Post Office Users' National Council (POUNC) related to mail matters. (POUNC *Annual Report* 1981-82, p. 33.)

[2] Sub-postmasters do Post Office work as agents and are paid on a scale reflecting the volume of work done. Crown offices are staffed by PO employees.

[3] Discussed below, pp. 17-19.

International comparisons

Before examining the arguments for removing the Post Office's monopoly of the letter and permitting private postal systems, we should note the compelling evidence that the British are better served by their Post Office than are many other industrialised countries by theirs. In March 1983, with understandable satisfaction, the Post Office issued a set of 'league tables' comparing its performance with that of nine other countries. The main features, summarised in Table 1, show that the UK has more post offices per head than any of the other countries except Ireland, and that the price of a first-class letter is in line with our European neighbours. The prices have been adjusted by the Post Office to take account of the differing costs of living among countries. This practice is open to question, particularly if the unadjusted prices are not given for comparison, but the main conclusions are clear.

Table 1:
Comparative Data on Selected Postal Administrations, 1983

	Post offices per 20,000 of population	Price[1] of an inland letter	Recent profit (loss or subsidy) £ million
	Number	Pence	
United Kingdom	8	15·5	91
Belgium	4	15·4	(220)
Denmark	5	12·2	(48)
Federal Germany	6	19·8	(930)
France	3	17·1	(320)
Greece	3	10·4	(5)
Italy	5	22·6	(481)
Ireland	13	22·9	(15)
Netherlands	4	16·7	(14)
USA	4	11·9	(800)

[1] Adjusted to take account of the differing costs of living among countries. Purchasing power parity figures from the Federal German statistics office.

Source: Post Office press release, March 1983.

The third column of Table 1 shows the British Post Office in outstanding light as the only one of 10 to make a profit. This is in marked contrast with both France and Federal Germany whose general industrial performance is often held to be more efficient.

Although comparisons of the *quality* of service provided are not easy, the achievement of the British Post Office in delivering 88 per cent of first-class mail the following (working) day probably exceeds that of most other administrations. Furthermore, in the UK there are two daily deliveries to urban addresses, which is very rare elsewhere; and in most other countries a significant proportion of mail is delivered to the garden gate or to a central collection point in blocks of flats and housing estates, or has to be collected from the local post office. In Federal Germany, for example, only 30 per cent is delivered to the front door.

Another significant benefit offered by the British system is the choice between first- and second-class speed of delivery. This was initiated by Mr Anthony Wedgwood Benn during his time as Postmaster General and replaced the distinction between ordinary mail and printed matter which still obtains in many other countries. Non-urgent items such as greetings cards, for example, must be sent at the full rate in systems which allow only printed matter at the cheaper rate.

Finally, the first weight step in the British letter tariff is 60 grams compared with 20 grams for all other countries in Table 1 except Ireland (60 g.) and the USA (28 g.).

Against such strong evidence that the British postal system is one of the best, what reasons are there for making a change?

THREE

Reasons for Change

Public dissatisfaction and Post Office tariffs

For a decade or more, many users of Post Office services—in particular such institutions as mail order houses—have criticised rising tariffs accompanied by declining standards of service. The criticisms appear to be borne out by Post Office data. Column (d) of Table 2 gives an index of postal tariffs after adjustment for inflation. Taking 1973 as 100, tariffs stood at 131·5 in 1982, thus substantially exceeding the rate of inflation over that decade. The main increase came in 1975 when the Post Office was released from a price freeze imposed by Mr Edward Heath's Conservative Government which had led to enormous losses. However, it should be noted that, if 1976 had been taken as the base year, tariffs in real terms would have been a little lower in 1981-82 than in 1975-76.

Table 2:
Indices of Monthly Earnings and Postal Tariffs (1973=100)

	Index of monthly earnings in transport and communications	Retail price index	Monthly earnings deflated by RPI	Postal tariff index adjusted for inflation
	(a)	(b)	(c)	(d)
1973	100·0	100·0	100·0	100·0
1974	117·8	110·4	106·7	98·1
1975	150·7	130·3	115·3	103·0
1976	170·6	162·4	105·0	137·3
1977	184·0	187·1	98·3	134·8
1978	208·1	213·3	97·6	127·1
1979	249·5	231·0	108·0	119·3
1980	298·2	267·5	111·5	115·8
1981	332·8	311·2	103·3	126·7
1982	364·0	347·0	104·9	131·5

Sources: (a) *Department of Employment Gazette*, adjusted 1973=100.
(b) and (d) *Post Office Report and Accounts, 1981-82*, p. 63.

Chart 1:
Indices of (1) Evaluated Post Traffic, (2) Postal Tariffs and (3) Average Monthly Earnings of Transport and Communication Workers, (2) and (3) adjusted for Inflation, 1973-82

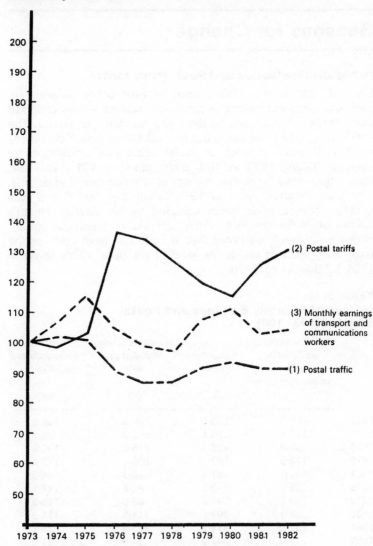

Sources: (1) (2) *Post Office Report and Accounts, 1981-82.*
(3) Department of Employment.

A second yardstick—more germane than the retail price index—can be used to analyse the increase in postal tariffs. About 93 per cent of postal costs consist of wages, pensions and national insurance contributions. Assuming for the moment that the services provided and productivity had remained unchanged, we would have expected postal tariffs to rise closely in line with wages.

Table 2 and Chart 1 show earnings in the nearest comparable sector: transport and communications. If during the period 1973-82 the Post Office had kept the quality of its services unchanged, had paid the going rate for labour in the market, and had passed on to the customer only the sector-average pay increases—no more and no less—postal tariffs would have mirrored movements in the earnings of transport and communications workers. Instead, as Chart 1 shows, postal tariffs went ahead. Since, as we shall see below, the services deteriorated somewhat in the period, we must conclude that the Post Office was paying its employees higher real wages (that is, allowing for inflation) than the labour market required but passing no benefit to the user. Thus the profits made in the past six years derive not from higher efficiency but from putting prices up faster than the rise in the cost of labour, whilst also reducing the quality of service. Further, the two main contributors to profits were the letter post, in which the Post Office has a legal monopoly, and the agency services,[1] in which it has an effective monopoly.

Quality of service

Selected indicators of the quality of services over the period 1972-73 to 1981-82 are given in Table 3. Without doubt, the standard which matters most to users is the speed and reliability of delivery. The first line of the Table shows that the speed of delivery of first-class mail was fairly steady at around 90 per cent 'next day' until 1979-80 when it fell sharply to 83 per cent. There was subsequently an improvement in the two most recent years. The delivery of second-class mail also reached a nadir in 1979-80, this being particularly significant since in 1975-76 the standard for 'on time' delivery was changed from within two working days of posting to three.

Moreover, in the decade covered, the Post Office has introduced a number of small changes which have enabled it to achieve a given standard of service more easily. For example,

---

[1] I.e., national savings, social security payments, vehicle, TV and other forms of licence, etc.

17

Table 3:
Selected Indicators of the Quality of the Postal Service, 1972/73 to 1981/82

	1972/73	1973/74	1974/75	1975/76	1976/77	1977/78	1978/79	1979/80	1980/81	1981/82
First-class letters delivered 'next day' (per cent)	92	89	89	92	93	93	88	83	86[g]	88
Second-class letters delivered 'on time' (per cent)	88[a]	85[a]	84[a]	89[a] 98[b]	96[b]	95[b]	89[b]	82[b]	92[b/g]	93[b]
Post Offices (No.)	24,132[c]	23,883[d]	23,660	23,390	23,124	22,921	22,793	22,639	22,475	22,405
Delivery points (thousands)	20,894	21,114	21,352	21,612	21,914	22,165	22,183	22,349	22,473	22,690
Collection points [e] (thousands)	100	100	100	100	100[f]	100	100	110	110	110
Sunday collection	YES	YES	YES	YES	NO[f]	NO	NO	NO	NO	NO

[a] Delivered within two working days of posting.

[b] Delivered within three working days of posting.

[c] This figure excludes 54 offices which have no public counter.

[d] This figure excludes 50 offices transferred to the Isle of Man administration.

[e] This refers to posting boxes and excludes many thousands of collections made from firms for which figures are not available.

[f] Sunday collections were suspended in May 1976.

[g] The figures shown refer to a Tuesday-to-Saturday sample until 1979/80; subsequently the sample is for the full week.

Source: Post Office.

latest collection times from boxes have become earlier and Sunday collection was ended in 1976-77.

The number of post offices has been reduced by over 7 per cent in the decade, though these were mostly small sub-offices doing little business. Such measures mask a further reduction in the standard of service. On the other hand, the number of delivery points has increased by 8·6 per cent and collection points by 10 per cent. The increases reflect new house building which, following the trend away from high-rise construction, has resulted in new housing estates with more front doors further apart.

If speed and reliability of delivery are taken as the touchstone of good postal service, the evidence points to a reduction of quality—though probably much less than the detractors of the Post Office claim. The increase in the number of collection and delivery points, invariably overlooked by the critics, must be recognised as offering some compensation. In general, it seems that residential users have done better out of the changes than has business.

Evidence which supports the trends revealed in Table 3 can be found in the 1981-82 Report of the Post Office Users' National Council (POUNC) which records that

'complaints . . . about postal delays declined for the second successive year. They are now at their lowest level for five years'. (p. 11).

Indeed, Annexe 2 of the Report shows that, in the years ending March 1981 and 1982, 'representations' of all kinds were almost 40 per cent lower than in 1980.

This conclusion is particularly interesting because, as may be seen in Chart 1, tariffs rose significantly in real terms in the last two recorded years while traffic remained level. The inference must be that users are willing to pay more for a better service. This runs counter to the Post Office's conventional wisdom which for years opted for reductions in the quality of service rather than the same or better service at a higher price. The mushrooming of independent courier services, examined later (pp. 30-32), also supports this inference.

Of the six indicators of quality of service shown in Table 3, most weight must be attached to the speed with which letters are delivered. Although this standard improved in the four years to 1981-82, it remains lower than in the preceding six years. Even allowing for the two indicators which *have* improved in the period covered—numbers of delivery and collection points—it still seems that the overall quality of the postal services has deteriorated.

Summary

To summarise, though the Post Office comes out extremely well on an international comparison, its prices have risen faster than its costs and the quality of its services has fallen. To that extent, public criticism is justified. Is it, however, sufficient reason to remove the letter monopoly, and indeed, privatise the Post Office? In 1970 I argued that the letter monopoly should be removed to test the Post Office's efficiency and its ability to compete with new entrants to the market.[1] While that argument still holds good, there is today an even stronger one. Not only is privatisation of the postal services desirable on both theoretical and practical grounds; it may also be essential for the survival of the Post Office as an institution.

---

[1] Ian Senior, *The Postal Service: Competition or Monopoly?*, Background Memorandum No. 3, IEA, 1970.

FOUR

Theoretical Considerations

The indefensible letter monopoly

In 1970 I argued that the Post Office's letter monopoly was unjustified by economic or any other logic.[1] Since then nothing has occurred to alter the force of the argument. In essence, a letter is nothing more than a thing-to-be-carried, like a newspaper or a parcel. That most letter packets contain information is immaterial since the carrier is paid for carrying and not for analysing the contents of the packet. The concept of a 'letter' is therefore an historical accident, and statutory monopolies world-wide have their roots primarily in commercial exploitation by governments of what was once the sole, and therefore inherently profitable, means of communication. No monopoly has been granted for the carriage of parcels, newspapers or any other thing-to-be-carried, and there is no ground whatever for singling out the 'letter'.

Indeed, nobody in the UK is quite sure what constitutes a 'letter'. The Post Office Act 1953 did not attempt to define it and instead used a catch-all:

> '... the expression "letter" includes a packet, so, however, as not to include a newspaper or a parcel unless a communication not forming part of a newspaper is contained therein'.[2]

Thus, the Post Office maintained at that time that the contents of the thing-to-be-carried, rather than its dimensions or weight, determined its status as a 'letter'. The absurdity of this position was recognised by Mr Wedgwood Benn who, as noted, abolished special concessions for printed mail and substituted a tariff differential offering the user a choice of speed of service. Mr Benn's logical appreciation of the unimportance of the contents of the thing-to-be-carried did not, however, extend to describing all such things as parcels. To have done so would have eliminated the letter monopoly overnight.

---

[1] *Ibid.*

[2] *Post Office Act 1953*, Chapter 36, HMSO, 1953, Section 3 (4).

A 'letter' defined

The British Telecommunications Act of 1981 defined a 'letter' as:

'any communication in written form which—
(a) is directed to a specific person or address;
(b) relates to the personal, private or business affairs of, or the business affairs of the employer of, either correspondent; and
(c) neither is to be nor has been transmitted by means of a telecommunication system,
and includes a packet containing any such communication'.[1]

Thus the original concept that a 'letter' is defined by its contents survives.

It is surprising that so significant a monopoly should have been sustained over the years by such weak and ill-founded legislation. It explains why, historically, the Post Office has threatened litigation to defend the monopoly more frequently than it has taken entrepreneurs to court.

It is worth noting that, for the following reasons, the 'letter' service does not constitute a natural or technical monopoly in economic terms:

- entry to the market by new suppliers is both cheap and simple, as the upsurge of courier companies in the past few years has demonstrated;
- postal services are labour-intensive and require few skills, so that new ones could quite easily be established from a large pool of unemployed workers;
- while there are economies of scale in handling postal traffic— a postman can deliver two letters to a house as cheaply as one—it is impossible to argue that a 'letter' monopoly would develop naturally, any more than in the distribution of parcels or milk.

It seems evident, therefore, that the Post Office's 'letter' monopoly has been maintained on grounds of pragmatic self-interest by successive governments which have used it as a source of revenue—as well as by the Post Office itself which has enjoyed the financial comfort it affords.

Cross-subsidisation of postal services

All governments since the war have stressed that cross-subsidising of services in public corporations misallocates resources and is therefore undesirable. Yet, as Table 4 shows, it is exactly what the Post Office has done. During the 10 years to 1981-82, the domes-

---

[1] *British Telecommunications Act 1981*, Chapter 38, HMSO, 1981, Section 66.

tic letter service and the overseas mail service (again, mainly letters) together made a profit of £101·3 million. As the next in importance, the agency services contributed £74·6 million, while the National Girobank, postal orders and services to telecommunications jointly contributed £18·8 million. All these profits derived from essentially monopoly services. By contrast, the one service run in competition with other carriers, including those in the private sector, performed disastrously: parcels recorded a cumulative loss of £151·2 million.

The arguments against cross-subsidisation are well known and do not need elaboration here. The only points to emphasise are the injustice of permitting the Post Office to provide a subsidised parcel service in competition with private carriers and the likely distortion of demand and misallocation of resources. That the parcel service has shown a profit in three out of the four most recent years after heavy losses earlier does credit to the Post Office's recent policy of more aggressive marketing, and raises the question why parcels were allowed to make losses for so long.

Unprofitable rural services

Although many public figures pay lip-service to the undesirability of cross-subsidising within nationalised industries, they defend the Post Office's letter monopoly as allowing profitable urban traffic to subsidise unprofitable rural mail. What is mistakenly regarded as the 'Rowland Hill principle' of uniform tariffs is held to be sacrosanct, although Hill never regarded it as such. As the Carter Committee noted,[1] Hill's view was simply that different rates should not be charged where this would overburden the system with administrative costs. If it can be shown that the system would *not* be overburdened by such rates, the argument for differential tariffs becomes overwhelming.

The often-repeated argument known as 'creaming off' is that, if the Post Office did not have a monopoly of the letter, private services would handle only profitable urban traffic, leaving the currently unprofitable rural traffic to the Post Office which would thus be forced into permanent loss.

This argument is circular, as will be demonstrated. The starting point for analysis, however, is that people make a choice where to live. In doing so they take into account an array of differing prices. In choosing to live in the countryside a rational person considers the cost of housing and transport first. He does not expect house prices in the country to be identical with those in town. Nor does

---

[1] *Report of the Post Office Review Committee,* Cmnd. 6850, HMSO, 1977.

Table 4:
Post Office's Profit (Loss) by Service, 1972-73 to 1981-82

£ Million

	1973	1974	1975	1976	1977	1978	1979	1980	1981	1982	Net Total 1973-1982
INLAND											
Letter services	(18·3)	(37·3)	(65·3)	20·0	26·4	21·3	14·1	16·8	18·5	57·2	53·4
Parcels	(17·5)	(25·3)	(44·8)	(42·8)	(18·0)	(7·7)	1·9	1·1	(5·2)	7·1	(151·2)
Registration	(1·0)	(1·7)	(3·2)	(0·5)	(0·2)	2·0	1·8	1·2	0·5	(1·3)	(2·4)
Other services	0·8	1·8	(1·7)	1·2	4·3	—	—	—	—	—	6·4
	4·3	4·9	(2·3)	7·9	5·6	8·9	6·9	0·2	1·5	10·0	47·9
Overseas	1·3	1·6	4·6	4·6	5·1	11·5	7·0	9·6	11·6	17·7	74·6
Agency services(a) Services to: National Girobank	0·5	0·5	2·7	(0·4)	1·1	2·5	0·5	0·3	0·1	0·8	⎱ 10·9
Postal orders	—	—	—	—	0·1	2·6	—	(0·6)	0·1	0·1	⎰
Services to telecommunications(b)	0·3	0·4	0·8	0·8	(0·1)	(0·7)	0·9	5·5	—	—	7·9
Interest on accumulated postal deficit	(12·9)	(2·4)	—	—	—	—	—	—	—	—	(15·3)
TOTAL	(42·5)	(57·5)	(109·2)	(9·2)	24·3	40·4	33·1	34·1	27·1	91·6	32·2

NOTE: Figures in brackets indicate a loss.

Source: Post Office Reports and Accounts, various years, statements B(S)2. When figures differ in different editions, data from the latest edition have been used.

(a) Listed in the note on page 17.

(b) E.g. delivery of telephone bills.

he expect to commute 20 miles to work by train for the same price as one stop on the bus. And nor does he expect that prices in his village shop—even for standard branded products—will be the same as in urban supermarkets. Why then, if he chooses a rural retreat with a long drive, should he expect—apparently as of right—to pay the same postage as another postal user who has opted to live in an accessible urban block of flats? People make decisions about location in the light of a set of price signals. There is no reason why *postal* price signals should be excluded.

A kind of 'social service'?

The argument for the Post Office's retention of the letter monopoly is often supported by the claim that letters constitute a form of 'social service' and that the Post Office has some quasi-moral duty to provide it. This was the approach of a report by the National Consumer Council in 1979—*Post Office, special agent* —the first chapter of which was devoted to how the Post Office could help to improve the take-up of welfare benefits and services. Most of the report's recommendations could be implemented quite cheaply—for example, the more effective display of DHSS leaflets at post office counters. The initial assumption, however, that the Post Office should be a 'social service' rather than a commercial operation remains unproven.

A further problem is that determining which services are 'social' depends on a value-judgement. A village post office may arguably provide a 'social' service, but so does the village pub and the village shop. No-one argues that there should be a state monopoly of the sale of beer for social service reasons. Another argument advanced is that letters and other postal services are 'essential' and therefore 'social'. Food, however, is much more essential yet nobody claims that Sainsburys should be compelled to open village stores where they do not exist so that people who have chosen to live in the country need not travel to the next village or town to shop.

Historically, the Post Office has cherished its rôle as provider of a universal 'social service' because this rôle has enabled it to retain the profitable letter monopoly. In short, the Post Office has embraced its obligation to serve rural communities as a way of keeping the monopoly.

The argument that dwellers in the decaying inner-city areas, should, through the postal system, unwittingly subsidise parts of the 'gin and Jag belt' in the Home Counties is obscure. If demo-cratically-elected government, either national or local, decides to subsidise the postal services of certain areas—say, the Western

Isles of Scotland—the providers of postal services, including the Post Office, could bid for the contract and the most efficient would win it. It seems logical that the source of funds for a local subsidy should be local since this would enable the costs to be borne by those who benefit from the subsidised service. Local councils wishing to retain deliveries in a particular rural area, for example, could provide a subsidy from the rates to any local contractor bidding to supply the service. If need be, a local referendum could be held to determine whether a subsidy was justified or wanted. Such a method would have the attraction of devolving decisions on 'social service' subsidies to those who would have to pay for them—and it would give them the right to refuse.

Transferring wealth from one group of citizens to another by taxation may be the proper function of democratic government. It is not, however, the function of the Post Office—nor indeed of any other trading concern, whether public or private.

We are therefore led to the following conclusions:

(i) There is no economic or social justification for the Post Office's 'letter' monopoly.

(ii) If the Post Office is deprived of the 'letter' monopoly, it must also be relieved of its obligation to supply all parts of the country at uniform prices (indeed, it would be under no obligation to provide a service anywhere and it would do so only if it expected to make a profit).

(iii) Except perhaps in very remote areas, rural services could be supplied with higher tariffs.

The prospect that even a few rural areas might be deprived of postal services condemns privatisation in the eyes of some critics. Yet we have already noted that, in extreme cases, government could pay a postal contractor to carry out otherwise unprofitable business. Moreover, the practical evidence set out below suggests that there is a surprisingly large volume of resources available to serve the postal market if permitted to do so. The prospect of unserved postal areas is therefore most unlikely, assuming suppliers are permitted a correct pricing structure and rational decision-making.

Breaking the circle?

The circularity of the populist argument for maintaining the letter monopoly can be summed up as follows:

- Urban services currently subsidise rural ones;
- the Post Office requires the 'letter' monopoly to continue this cross-subsidisation;

- the 'letter' monopoly enables the Post Office to charge uniform tariffs;
- uniform tariffs enable urban services to subsidise rural ones.

And so on *ad infinitum*. Yet the circularity of the argument can be broken the moment it is demonstrated that there is no justification for urban to subsidise rural services at all.

An economist would phrase the arguments differently but would reach the same conclusions. In this instance, the reasoning would be as follows:

- if there were no statutory monopoly of the 'letter', competition would ensue and the prices charged by all contractors would reflect their costs;
- people whose value-judgements led them to discern 'social' costs and benefits not captured by the pricing systems of commercial operators should be given the opportunity, through democratic channels, to correct the apparent failure of the market through subventions on 'social' grounds;
- in order to prevent a misallocation of resources, subventions should be voted by those most closely affected and most willing to pay.

When the argument is expressed thus it becomes clear that the onus for demonstrating the 'social' costs and benefits of postal services falls upon those arguing for subvention. To date, reasoned argument on this issue has been conspicuously lacking.

FIVE

New Postal Services

Historical suppression of competition

In the UK and elsewhere there have been repeated attempts, some successful and of considerable duration, to operate a postal service in competition with that of the state. The majority have been suppressed in one way or another by government. Among the most successful in the UK were William Dockwra's London Penny Post of 1680 which had 400 receiving points and provided house-to-house service. It was put out of business by the government following a long court case. In 1709 Charles Povey introduced a service at a charge of only one-halfpenny, thereby undercutting the General Post Office. He introduced bellmen who collected post on the street, an idea later taken up by the GPO. In 1887 Richard King launched his company, Boy Messengers Limited, and was able to muster enough support from Parliament and the press to force the GPO to grant him a licence. Indeed, it introduced its own messenger service to compete.[1]

In this century, a number of less ambitious services have been suppressed—such as those run by some of the Oxford colleges —which could hardly have been considered a serious threat to the Post Office.

At various times private postal services have been started in the USA, Australia and Holland by entrepreneurs who found loopholes in the law; they have proved successful, particularly when account is taken of the precarious nature of their existence.

That there should be determined efforts to provide competing postal services indicates that entrepreneurs believe they could do better than the state monopoly. They have inevitably begun with the most profitable inter-urban traffic, thus re-inforcing the 'creaming-off' argument. Yet it is precisely because state postal administrations make excess profits on the urban traffic that competitors enter that part of the market. If the administrations made profits over the whole network by differential pricing, competition would also be spread over the network.

---

[1] For a fuller account, Robert Carnaghan, 'Free enterprise in the postal services', *Freedom First*, No. 71, June 1972.

Private letter services during the 1971 strike

On 20 January 1971, the postmen went on strike. Two days previously Mr Christopher Chataway, then Minister of Posts and Telecommunications, announced that private postal services would be allowed to operate *under licence* for the duration of the strike. This momentous decision meant that, for the first time since 1591, a government had voluntarily relinquished its monopoly over letters. The result was quite remarkable. Within a matter of days no fewer than 562 services had been licensed up and down the country, and others were doubtless operating without a licence.

Many of these operations were intended more to print what philatelists call 'Cinderella' stamps than to carry mail, but some were unquestionably serious operations. One of them, Randall's Mail Service, charged substantially more than the Post Office's letter rate of 3p, yet at the end of the six-week strike claimed to have handled about half a million items.[1]

Perhaps even more remarkable was the speed with which some of these *ad hoc* services linked up during the strike into a network called the Association of Mail Services. In very little time, local services were finding ways to expand their areas of operation.

A further interesting aspect was the attitude of the public which, assuming the claims of the operators were reasonably accurate, was prepared to entrust quite large quantities of mail to completely unknown firms, makeshift in the extreme and with no possible future beyond the end of the strike. How much more would it have been willing to entrust to established firms entering the market-place with genuine prospects of staying there!

Private parcel services

Historically, the main carriers of parcels have been the Post Office, British Rail and the road services. The latter have at times been partly nationalised. For many years until 1979 the Post Office's parcel service made losses, frequently large, and the other carriers in the state sector claimed their services were also unprofitable. Nevertheless, new private services have entered the market in the past decade as an extension partly of security services and partly of courier services.

For the security services, it was by no means an obvious move. Their system of armoured vans was developed to move small numbers of high-value units between a limited number of points.

---

[1] *Daily Telegraph*, 12 March 1971.

By contrast, a parcel service requires cheaper (non-armour-plated) vans to move large numbers of low-value items flexibly between very many points. It might have seemed, therefore, that the security services would start with the wrong structure of vehicles and staff and would compete only at the margin by using unnecessarily expensive equipment at times when it would otherwise be idle. Yet, in practice, these services have extended their scope into nationwide coverage. They charge more than the Post Office but generally offer a faster service.

One example is Security Express which has recently collaborated with the Rymans chain to provide parcel collecting points. Its basic charge is £6 per address for delivery plus 60p per kilogram up to a limit of 36 kg. per parcel. Although these charges are higher than those of the Post Office, which begin at £1·20 per kilogram for nationwide delivery, the Security Express service offers some important advantages. These are:

— next-day delivery;
— door-to-door collection and delivery;
— identification by a code number of every parcel going through the system, enabling them to be traced if necessary.

The last of these advantages may counterbalance the modest compensation for loss which Security Express offers—up to £20 compared with up to £300 offered by the Post Office.

A comparison of the different services supplied by the two systems does not immediately suggest that either is superior. Indisputably, however, the range of choice to the consumer is being extended. Moreover, it is noteworthy that the private sector is increasing its activity in what used to be considered an unprofitable market.

The courier services

A remarkable phenomenon over the past decade has been the emergence of a large number of courier services in London and the main cities. It was at one time thought that such services would infringe the Post Office's 'letter' monopoly. In February 1972, for example, a courier service was launched in London by an enterprising Australian, Richard King, who presumably had been impressed by operations which had started during the postal strike the preceding year. King's 'Post-Haste' service offered delivery in four hours within an area of London covering the law courts, Parliament and the Strand using a team of 10 motorcyclists constituted as a co-operative of self-employed. The Post Office immediately threatened King with legal proceedings. Customers were doubtless afraid they might be accused of abetting King if they used an illegal service, and it was thus short-lived.

Public frustration with the Post Office's service increased during the early 1970s, particularly concerning the unreliability of delivery within the big cities. It became common for urgent letters or packages to be sent by taxi—an extremely inefficient use of resources. Quite soon after the demise of 'Post-Haste', other courier services were launched using motor-bikes controlled from a central point by radio. The Post Office threatened legal proceedings but took none of the operators to court. In a matter of months their number had mushroomed and by 1975 there were probably 30-50 such services in London alone. Since then their number has probably fluctuated in that range.

The courier services exploited the loop-hole in the law discovered by Richard King. The law permitted people to employ agents (couriers) to collect and deliver individual letters, though not to collect them on a generalised basis. Thus, the couriers could collect items from individual addresses on request but could not install public collection boxes.

It was to meet this new competition that, in March 1976, the Post Office launched its own variant called 'Expresspost'. In many respects the service was an imitation of the couriers and its price was a little lower. Since then it has been widely extended and now covers more than 60 major conurbations using a special fleet of vans, inter-city rail links, the Post Office's underground railway in London and a fleet of radio-controlled motor-cycles. 'Expresspost' has been heavily promoted in the media, including prime television time, with resources far beyond the means of individual private couriers whose marketing is very limited.

Yet, despite the Post Office's overwhelming strength—compared even with the combined total of *all* the private couriers— the latter have survived and, it would seem, prospered. More importantly, their legitimacy has now been recognised in law. On 16 October 1981, the then Secretary of State for Industry, Mr Patrick Jenkin, laid before Parliament an order suspending the Post Office's letter monopoly to permit time-sensitive mail to be delivered by private carriers provided they charge a minimum fee, then set at £1 per letter. This was the first real relaxation of the monopoly, other than during the postal strike, for a century or more.

The significance of the couriers is two-fold. First, they are a classic example of private enterprise recognising a demand overlooked by a state monopoly and satisfying it to the benefit of the community. Secondly, it demonstrates that the private sector can compete successfully with the Post Office in the provision of postal services. It is remarkable that the private couriers have not been eliminated by 'Expresspost'. Not only does the Post Office have huge resources; for years it has also had only the most rudimentary internal accounting system, though this is now being improved. The lack of accurate accounting meant that in the early years of 'Expresspost' only the marginal costs would have been known—the number of new staff and vehicles required, for example; the allocation of overheads would have been sketchy. No financial details about the service are given in the Post Office's reports and accounts, although even the minor service of postal orders has its own profit-and-loss account, balance sheet and statement of reserves. The private courier services have had to function as profitable enterprises or else they would have gone bankrupt. 'Expresspost' may be profitable, *but it does not have to show a profit*. It could well be subsidised by other services, not least by the letter monopoly, and this cross-subsidy would not appear in the accounts. The 'Expresspost' service is now seven years old and the Post Office's annual accounts could be expected to set out its financial performance.

Conclusion

From all the evidence reviewed in this section it is clear that the private sector wishes to compete with the Post Office and, when permitted to do so, successfully introduces new or specialised services which satisfy particular users' wants. Historically, the Post Office has tried to eliminate competition by legal or other devices. When it has failed, it has on occasions resorted to imitating the private sector. It is evident that competition in the postal service, limited though it has been to date, has benefited society and should therefore be extended.

SIX

Implementation

Removal of the letter monopoly

In my 1970 IEA paper I put the case for removing the Post Office's letter monopoly. *The Economist* supported this view, saying that '. . . it is absurd that the Post Office should have a monopoly to carry letters in Britain . . .'[1] The Liberal MP, Mr Richard Wainwright, also agreed in a notable contribution to a debate in 1975 when he called for the removal of the monopoly and for local pilot experiments in competition.[2]

The Carter Committee in 1977 was critical of the Post Office's cavalier attitude to its customers.

> 'Sometimes its customers get the feeling that they are being graciously permitted to use the systems . . . From the evidence we have seen and heard, we fear that the Post Office knows too little about its customers . . .'[3]

Astonishingly, the Committee later concluded that the solution was to strengthen the letter monopoly and to have 'more frequent prosecution of offenders'![4]

Mrs Thatcher's first administration took power in 1979 dedicated to returning some nationalised industries to private enterprise. Yet, though there were hints from her first Secretary of State for Industry, Sir Keith Joseph, that the Post Office's monopoly might be abolished, the legitimising of courier services has been complemented by only one modest reform permitting charitable organisations, such as the Scouts, to deliver Christmas cards.

A possible explanation of that Government's timidity is that the Post Office is still seen as a source of public revenue and is required to make a contribution to government funds. For, in the past seven years, the Post Office accumulated a cash surplus of £104 million which the 1979-83 Government did not permit it to spend on its investment programme—a form of compulsory saving which therefore reduces the public sector borrowing requirement.

---

[1] *Economist*, 5 December 1970.
[2] *Hansard*, 15 July 1975, col. 1,357ff.
[3] *Report of the Post Office Review Committee*, July 1977, p. 42.
[4] *Ibid.*, p. 71.

It is difficult to think of a cogent reason why any government should not remove the monopoly, other than short-term financial expediency. And even this reason would be invalidated if the Post Office were to be sold to the public.

The Post Office plc

There has been a succession of reforms over the past 20 years intended to make the Post Office more commercial, more free from political interference, and more responsive to its users' wants. This process, which began in 1964 when Mr Wedgwood Benn was Postmaster General, resulted in the Post Office becoming a public corporation in 1969 and losing its ministerial head. The residual sponsor, the Ministry of Posts and Telecommunications, was short-lived and its main responsibility passed to the Department of Industry. During the 1970s, the postal functions were increasingly separated from telecommunications at local, regional and headquarters levels. The complete separation of the two services was achieved in 1981. The time is now ripe to take the next logical step of selling the Post Office to the public.

The prime reason for this final step is that it would be in the interest of both users and the Post Office itself. At present, users —who comprise virtually every member of the public as well as institutions like mail order houses—have no effective say in the Post Office's operations. The Post Office Users' National Council is a toothless watchdog[1] set up to look after users' interests when the Post Office became a corporation. It has the right to be *consulted* about proposed changes in services, and its 25 or so members are appointed by the government. The intention is that they should have a wide variety of backgrounds and be able to give a good spread of users' views. In addition, there are equivalent councils for Scotland, Wales and Northern Ireland and about 200 Post Office advisory committees throughout the country. Members of the latter are drawn from local authorities, commercial organisations and local voluntary bodies.

It is not to be expected that this elaborate structure of advice can achieve the same results as competition. We have already seen, for example, that the Post Office launched its 'Expresspost' service in 1976 under the spur of competition from the private courier services—and not as a consequence of pressure from the advisory councils and committees.

Nor is it clear that the POUNC's reports on proposed tariff

---

[1] The POUNC's annual report for 1981-82 contains a cartoon of POUNC, smiling and benign, with no teeth visible, but bearing the title 'watchdog'.

changes genuinely achieve what users want—not least because different users may have differing and even contradictory requirements. It is even likely that Post Office managers, knowing that whatever they recommend will be whittled down by the Council, ask for more than they want in order to be able to make concessions. Moreover, the success of the new parcel and courier services proves that in some cases there is significant public demand for better service at *higher* prices, whereas the users' representative bodies have invariably fought for the continuation of the same service at similar or lower prices. The prognostication of Mr Ian Mikardo, MP, in 1968 when the users' councils were being set up seems to have been fulfilled:

> 'I doubt very much whether all this great apparatus will be worthwhile— whether the game will be worth the candle and whether it will justify the benefit to the consumer'.[1]

The Carter Committee recognised the problem of accountability to users but came up with such inappropriate solutions as more international comparisons and more power to the users' councils. The weakness of the Committee's analytical powers can be seen from the following statement:

> '. . . the Post Office has as its prime duty a responsibility to its customers —*who in their capacity as citizens are also its owners* . . .'[2]

The hallmark of ownership is control and the only citizens who have some form of control over the Post Office are the responsible ministers and officials at the Department of Industry. The idea that private individuals own the Post Office at present is ludicrous. It stands in stark contrast to my proposal that individuals should be given the opportunity of true ownership. If ownership is thought desirable, privatisation is the only solution.

The Post Office is currently profitable and has good prospects of remaining so even without the 'letter' monopoly because it has a national network, specialised equipment, trained staff and experience accumulated over a century or more. If shares in it were offered to the public we would expect them to be taken up. In particular, major users such as the mail order houses would have the opportunity to buy enough shares to gain seats on the board of directors. Individual users with axes to grind could also buy shares and have the forum of annual general meetings to voice their views.

Post Office executives and other staff would be encouraged to

---

[1] *Hansard*, 11 November 1968, col. 64.

[2] *Op. cit.*, p. 17 (my italics).

hold shares in the company, perhaps offered at a discount during the transition from nationalised industry status. The outlook of Post Office managers has long been criticised as bound by rule-books dating back to the days when the Post Office was part of the Home Civil Service. To judge by several successful 'management buy-outs', we may hope that they would welcome the opportunity to share in the profits and capital value created by their efforts.

Counter Services plc

As has been noted, postal services have already been fully separated from telecommunications on the ground that they were two heterogeneous operations. The same logic applies with equal force to the difference between counter services and the mail. The mail service consists of carrying physical objects, while the counter service is concerned with money transactions. Both services will change beyond recognition in the coming decade. Letters written on paper will be replaced by the 'electronic letter' (discussed below, pp. 45-46), and the Post Office's paper-based banking, money transfer and agency services will be transformed by automated teller machines, point-of-sale registers, home banking, and a variety of electronic systems for transferring funds based on plastic cards.

Although the electronic revolution will lie behind the development of both services, its application will be so different to each that they will require freedom to progress independently. In particular, since the counter services will increasingly compete with other financial institutions and the mail service with private operators, it will be desirable to prevent any form of cross-subsidisation between the two services—as there was between posts and telecommunications when they were combined.

The logic of separating the mail from the counter services into two independent companies can be seen by analysing counter transactions. Table 5 shows that the sale of postage stamps (which includes acceptance of parcels) and postage meter sales account for only 30 per cent of counter transactions. Agency services account for 53 per cent, 14 per cent are funds transfers (either by the dying postal order service or the more vital National Girobank), and the remaining 3 per cent are National Savings and gift tokens. Thus, 70 per cent of counter transactions constitute a form of retail banking.

Postage stamps could be sold anywhere. At present very few shops—other than sub-post offices—sell them because the Post Office refuses to allow them a margin for doing so. There is no

Table 5:
Post Office Counter Services, 1981-82

	Transactions	
	millions	*per cent*
Postal services		
– Sales of postage stamps	670[a]	29
– Postage meter sales	26[a]	1
Transfer of funds		
– National Girobank	239	10
– Postal orders issued	88	4
National Savings Bank and gift tokens	67	3
Other agency services	1,250	53
	2,340	100

[a] Author's estimate.

Source: Post Office Report and Accounts, 1981-82, p. 65.

reason in principle why postage stamps should not be sold at all retail outlets. Separately constituted, a new Counter Services plc could continue to sell stamps and accept parcels for the Post Office, but on an agency basis.

For many years the Post Office's counter services have enjoyed a *de facto* monopoly over a wide range of government agency services. An example is the payment of pensions and social security. This monopoly, which has always provided the Post Office with a guaranteed margin of profit, is, however, also being eroded since many forms of benefit are now paid directly into individual bank accounts at lower cost to the government and more convenience to the recipients. The next logical step must be for banks and building societies to be invited to tender in competition with the Post Office to provide other services, such as the issue of vehicle licences.

It is not certain that the banks would want to compete for this business. Their high street premises are more lavish than the typical down-at-heel post office and carry higher overheads. In 1982 the big clearing banks quoted about 30p as the average cost of a counter transaction, whereas the Post Office's counter services carried out 2,340 million transactions at an average cost of 22p each. Even though, on this evidence, Counter Services plc might expect to retain government business, the threat of competition from other financial institutions would remain a powerful spur to maintaining lower costs.

It is noticeable that Post Office counters are already becoming more commercial in outlook and are collaborating with the private sector. In March 1983, for example, an agreement was concluded with the Leicester Building Society to open and operate the Society's accounts at Post Office counters nationwide. Moreover, a Post Office spokesman has made it clear that similar arrangements could be made with other building societies. A further demonstration of how the Post Office's attitude is changing also occurred in March 1983 when prominent advertisements appeared in the national press offering 'Country music—at your post office—as seen on TV'!

Now that the Post Office's counter service is at last beginning to recognise the necessity to compete with other institutions, there seems even stronger logic in giving it the freedom to do so as a separate limited liability company.

SEVEN

Likely Developments

Urban services

The removal of the Post Office's 'letter' monopoly does not require legislation. The government could simply announce it was issuing an open general licence to all-comers to provide letter services, as it did during the 1971 strike. New postal services would quickly come into being. The most likely serious contenders would be the providers of parcel services such as Securicor and Security Express. Their rôle in particular might be to provide national trunk networks linking local collection and delivery companies. Other candidates would be the courier services and the milk distributors. Because of the Post Office's existing tariff structure, it is almost inevitable that these new services would initially concentrate on urban areas. Many would be essentially local operations, though the experience of 1971 suggests they would soon collaborate to extend their coverage.

Faced with competition from lower local tariffs, the Post Office would be compelled to cut the cost of urban mail. It has already had to do this with parcels. It would then have to find ways either of cutting the costs of rural services or of increasing tariffs for rural mail in order to compensate for the revenue lost in the towns. If it did introduce a differential tariff structure, private operators would see new prospects in rural areas and would extend their activities.

Rural services

The collection and delivery of mail, particularly delivery, are more expensive in rural areas because distances are greater and the density of population, and hence postal traffic, is lower. The Post Office has for years accepted the necessity of providing poorer service to rural areas, which have fewer post offices, fewer collection boxes and only one delivery per day. If rural services are to be made profitable, either their pattern will have to be changed or they will have to be priced more highly, or a mixture of the two. A number of obvious economies could be made in deliveries, such as boxes at the end of drives—a standard practice in many countries. For the collection of mail, private boxes could be rented at the local sorting office. There might also be fewer collections and deliveries.

The alternative approach is the introduction of a two-tier price structure. Letters posted in designated rural boxes would bear a surcharge. This would be eminently reasonable since the rural dweller would thus be paying for his choice of location. It would also be possible for the Post Office or other carrier to introduce a surcharge on mail posted *to* rural areas. Rural addresses would have a special prefix in their postal codes to inform the *sender* that he must include a surcharge in the postage. Letters not bearing the surcharge stamps would be readily identified at the rural office of collection or delivery. Then either the addressee could be required to pay the surcharge—as currently occurs with understamped mail—or the item could be downgraded from first- to second-class mail.

Although a differential tariff structure would be criticised for being more complicated than the present simple system, it would allocate costs of postal work more correctly between users.

Sharing the revenue

Interconnection between competing postal operations would require different accounting systems to apportion revenue than the Post Office currently uses. This is not a weighty criticism. There are, for example, several hundred small telecommunications systems in the USA in parallel with the giant Bell network. All are interconnected and have to share the revenue from any call which is connected across two or more systems.

For letters, there are three main stages:

(i) local collection and sorting;

(ii) intermediate transport in bags;

(iii) local sorting and delivery.

As has already been indicated, local companies could undertake the first and third stages and national companies the second. The inter-company tariff could be set according to the very simple criterion of the weight of a bag handled.

It is worth recalling in this context the Rowland Hill concept that different rates should not be charged where they would *overburden the system with administrative costs*. The new postal services would have to keep some form of traffic records for accounting purposes and the cost of doing so would have to be covered by its tariffs. These would still have to be competitive with those of the privatised Post Office which until now has had no form of financial accounting system for local managers. Thus, being unable to show a profit, they have had no incentive to take profitable action. This, more than anything else, explains the poor management style of the past. The notion that an enterprise can be run successfully without records and accounts of its output is absurd. It is hard to accept that the mail system would be 'over-burdened' by the cost of accounting.

International mail

International mail would probably be handled initially by the Post Office plc which has a well-tried network and, historically, has made a good profit on this side of its operations. There are already, however, a number of established international courier companies operating regular services to main cities abroad, and they would be expected to increase the scope of their activities.

Counter services

In the early days of the newly-privatised Counter Services plc, changes in the counter services would be less marked. Fewer stamps would be sold because they would be available from other outlets and because the private mail services would have captured some of the traffic. Fewer parcels might be received if the new operators extended their service into carrying them. New agencies would open to receive both the letters and parcels of the new operators, as Rymans already accepts Security Express parcels.

On the other hand, the counters would have to adapt under the impact of the technological revolution in transferring funds. The Post Office's chain of 22,405 counters is twice the size of the branch network of the four main clearing banks combined. Yet, technologically, it has fallen far behind the banks. It offers no automated teller machines to dispense cash and provide other services outside counter service hours; it is not experimenting with the transfer of funds electronically at the point of retail sale, as are the banks; nor is it experimenting with home banking through the Prestel network, as is one enterprising building society. Its clerks still use the backs of envelopes for computations as though electronic calculators did not exist. Only recently, at eight post offices, has the first experiment begun in using an electronic register to record transactions and balance at the end of the day.

Indeed, the Post Office's counter services are in grave danger of becoming technologically obsolete. It need not be concerned about its 20,832 sub-offices because they are paid on a scale of fees according to the business they do. The 1,573 crown offices would, however, remain. Many are likely to become redundant under the impact of home banking and other technological developments unless they diversify their activities to justify the high costs of prime high street sites.

A clue to the future of the crown offices is to be found in their initiative, already mentioned, to become an ordering point for a special pop-record offer. They will increasingly require new activities of this sort if they are to meet the costs of their sites, and it seems much more likely that local managers would seek out profitable new activities if they worked for a private company responsive to the competitive disciplines of the market. Equally, if the crown offices remained state-owned as at present, it would be wrong to allow them to offer retailing and other services in competition with the private sector since they could be subsidised by profits from captive agency services for central government. In short, to ensure its survival, the Post Office's counter network must be hived off to the private sector.

Surprisingly, it is possible that the future of rural post offices is more secure than that of urban. If the Post Office were to lose its letter monopoly, it is unlikely that many rural post offices would be affected—for two reasons. First, sub-postmasters are paid on a scale of fees representing the work they do. This is measured accurately because all their materials, such as postal orders, vehicle licences and so on, are supplied from the local head post office. The Post Office is therefore already able to adjust the payments it makes to the value of the work performed, and would have no strong incentive to close offices even if their output fell. Secondly, when a sub-postmaster retires or wishes to give up his agency, it is common for the Post Office to have to choose between a number of applicants anxious to take it on. If a village has no post office, it is generally because the Post Office refuses to appoint a sub-postmaster and seldom because no-one is willing to take on the agency. Indeed, it is possible that, under the spur of competition, the Post Office would appoint *more* sub-postmasters. (The giant petrol companies supply even the most remote areas of the country.)

EIGHT

Timing

Inelastic demand for postal services

Now is an opportune time for transforming the Post Office into two private companies. As Table 4 showed, all services are currently operating at a profit apart from registration (a small loss). A much more important aspect, however, is the longer-term future of the Post Office's services. Chart 1 showed that the index of evaluated postal traffic has been steady since 1976-77, after falling sharply following the savage tariff increases of the previous year. Table 6 gives further traffic data, including calculations of the price elasticity of demand[1] for postal traffic. In essence, when there are few, if any, substitutes for a good or service, demand for it is generally price-inelastic and lies between 0 and -1. To take a simple example, if elasticity is exactly -1, demand will fall by 5 per cent when the price increases by 5 per cent.

Every supplier of goods and services hopes to face an inelastic demand for his product, because this enables him to raise prices with little if any loss of sales. The Table suggests that the price inelasticity of demand for postal services is still much less than unity—that is, demand is inelastic.

Some caution is required in interpreting the elasticity calculations shown in Table 6. To begin with, they take no account of influences on demand for postal services other than price—such as the level of activity in the economy generally and the actions of competitors, including other parcel services and telecommunications. Nor do they attempt to explain the lagged effects of price changes, for which quarterly data would be needed. These influences all contribute to the relationship between changes in tariffs and changes in mail carried, and they explain why the price elasticity of demand appears to fluctuate from one year to the next. In the series of elasticity calculations, however, 1976 and 1981 are particularly interesting. Those years saw large tariff increases of 33 per cent and 9·5 per cent respectively, yet the

---

[1] The price elasticity of demand measures the relationship between a rise (or fall) in price and the fall (or rise) in demand.

Table 6:
Mail Carried, Tariff Index and Price Elasticity of Demand, 1972-73 to 1981-82

	1973	1974	1975	1976	1977	1978	1979	1980	1981	1982
(1) Inland letter traffic index, volume (1973=100)	100	102	100	91	86	87	91	94	92	92
(2) Overseas letter traffic index, volume (1973=100)	100	106	110	107	103	110	107	102	93	84
(3) Evaluated(a) traffic index (1973=100)	100	102	101	91	87	87	92	94	92	92
(4) Tariff index adjusted for inflation	100	98	103	137	135	127	119	116	127	132
(5) Price elasticity of demand (as explained in the note to p. 00) derived from (3) and (4)		−1·1	−0·2	−0·3	(b)	0	−0·9	−0·8	−0·2	0

(a) Consolidated measure of mails volume reflecting the different workloads in handling letters and parcels.

(b) Calculation shows a positive elasticity which is not meaningful.

Sources: (1)-(4) Post Office Report and Accounts, 1981-82.
(5) Author's calculations.

impact on traffic was such as to produce a low elasticity calculation of −0·2 to −0·3. This supports the contention that demand for mail services is still relatively insensitive to tariff increases.

Electronic mail and the new services

How long the demand for traditional mail services will remain insensitive to price is a matter for conjecture. Certainly, the next decade will see the widespread development of electronic mail and a major decline in paper mail.

Electronic mail is a message which at some stage in transmission becomes an electronic signal instead of remaining a piece of paper from first to last. The sorting and carriage of paper is infinitely more demanding of resources than the transmission and switching of an electronic current. Several forms of electronic 'letter' are already on the market, including telex and facsimile services. The next stage will be the receipt of messages into the home *via* the television set or personal computer.

British Telecom's Prestel is a forerunner of this concept. British Leyland's Comet is an example of a switched network for business use which could well be extended into the home. And a new system based on home computers has recently been launched called Micronet. The common feature of such services is that paper is eliminated throughout all switching and transmission stages. Paper is unnecessary as an input unless a facsimile is being transmitted, and it is unnecessary as an output unless a permanent record is required.

The Post Office is aware of this threat to its very existence and has therefore launched two electronic letter services of its own. One, Intelpost, is a public international facsimile service. It began operating in 1980 between London and Toronto and has since been extended to cover 100 towns and cities in the UK and abroad. Its network is also available for those with their own facsimile equipment and transmission is, of course, *via* networks of the British Telecom and foreign telecommunications administrations.

The second service, known as Electronic Post, is for bulk mailings. These are transmitted electronically between selected centres in the UK, printed by laser (with letter heads and signature included), inserted into envelopes, and introduced into the mail stream for normal delivery. The service is currently on trial between London and Manchester where it can already reach seven million addresses; four more centres are planned.

It is only a matter of time before every home in the country will be equipped to receive electronic letters. The advent of cable television and direct communication *via* satellites and roof-top dish aerials will provide new means of transmission to hasten the advent of this revolutionary medium.

The future therefore holds the challenge of competition for the Post Office, whether the letter monopoly is removed or not. With the new liberal climate for telecommunications and the revolution in information technology, whether the Post Office retains a monopoly of the paper letter will ultimately become irrelevant because it has no rights over the electronic letter. If the Post Office is to compete in the new high-technology communications industry, it must learn to compete *now* in a traditional industry in which it is still the acknowledged leader, both nationally and even internationally. Furthermore, competition would have the merit of making traditional postal services as efficient as possible during the transition to electronic mail.

NINE

Benefits of Privatised Postal Services

For the consumer

The changes which would follow the abolition of the letter monopoly and the creation of Post Office plc and Counter Services plc would be of clear benefit to the urban and the major commercial users of postal services. Urban postal tariffs would fall and the quality of service would rise under the impact of competition. New flexible services, such as those of the couriers, would be offered. If the user was dissatisfied with the Post Office's service, he would seek out a competitor. If no competitor eventually emerged for a given type of service, the Post Office would have proved that what it was offering was as efficient as possible in the context.

Rural users already endure a worse service than urban users—with fewer deliveries, collections and post offices. With the Post Office's monopoly and uniform pricing, the rural user has no means of obtaining a better service even if he is willing to pay more for it. The present system ensures that, in the absence of competition, rural dwellers' wants and preferences *cannot* be reflected in the service provided and the price paid. In particular, rural dwellers might wish to see the network of rural post offices expanded, even if transactions in them cost a little more than in urban offices. If services to some especially remote communities could not be provided profitably by commercial operators, local government councils could offer them subsidies and invite bids to supply the services, thus ensuring that the most efficient won the contract. Given the advent of the 'electronic letter', subsidies of this sort should last only a few years.

Taking urban and rural users together, it seems clear that there would be a net benefit from the introduction of competition and the responsiveness to users' requirements which it brings. Commercial users—the mail order houses, in particular—should welcome the chance to buy shares in a privatised Post Office plc, which would enable them to influence its operations.

For Post Office staff

It is unfortunate that, for some time, the Post Office has seen the removal of its letter monopoly as a *threat*, held over it by government to ensure its compliance. Instead, the removal of the monopoly coupled with freedom to set tariffs and to supply only profitable services should be seen as a particularly attractive reward to its staff for making the Post Office both commercial and efficient by international standards.

Post Office managers must be justifiably irritated by any government which compels them to deposit the Corporation's profits with the Treasury instead of using them to develop the business. Indeed, it was just such a short-sighted policy which starved the telecommunications business of investment during the 1960s and 1970s.

It is 14 years since the Post Office ceased to be a civil service department and a new generation of managers is now reaching the top. Its marketing has become far more aggressive and many new services have been started in the past two years or so. The new managers have only to look at the remarkable success of the National Freight Corporation since it was handed back to the private sector through a management buy-out to see the strength of their position.

Postmen and counter clerks have long cherished the Post Office's monopoly status and they might therefore initially oppose the proposed changes. This would be a short-sighted reaction which ignores their longer-term interests. As already indicated, the paper letter will come under increasing threat from the 'electronic letter', and the traditional paper-based transfer of funds will rapidly be replaced by new electronic methods including home banking. *The jobs of all postmen and all counter clerks are therefore already at risk from the new technologies.* Thus, the protective monopoly which they have considered valuable hitherto is becoming irrelevant with the march of science and technology. The question for all Post Office staff, therefore, is whether they have a better chance of surviving in a competitive world if they begin to work in a privatised concern *now*, or if they cling to an outmoded historical status until it is too late.

For the country

The revolution in information technology is just beginning, but it is already eliminating the boundaries between computers, telephone exchanges, typewriters and television sets, and between banks, building societies and other financial institutions. It is creating an unprecedented climate of competition. The British may be less good at manufacturing than the Germans and Japanese; but we excel in the provision of services. The Post Office is a provider of services. It does not require the crutch of an archaic and near-obsolete monopoly. It requires the spur of rivalry as a privately-owned company competing with others. The benefits to the British people would be considerable if we were permitted to enjoy competing and privatised postal and counter services.

Some IEA Papers on Nationalised Industries

Hobart Paper 95
Transport without Politics . . . ?
A study of the scope for competitive markets in road, rail and air
John Hibbs   1982   £2·50

'Out today is a provoking little pamphlet with the hopeful, if impractical title of "Transport without Politics? . . .".

'It takes the arguments current at the time of the last rail strike about introducing the fresh air of competition into the State rail system much further. It calls for a national corporation to take over the road system—reminding us of the British Roads idea once backed by Lord Marsh when he headed British Rail—and eventually the rail network to help decentralise the railway system.

'Ahead of its time, of course, but this year's rail strike has triggered off much new thinking about the future shape, and cost, of transport in Britain. Some of this book's ideas may be a bit closer than the NUR or ASLEF think.'
                                   Leith McGrandle—*Daily Express*

Hobart Paper 89
What Future for British Coal?
Optimism or realism on the prospects to the year 2000
Colin Robinson and Eileen Marshall   1981   £2·00

'. . .this Hobart Paper makes a valuable contribution to the debate on Britain's energy policy.'   *Financial Times*, in an Editorial

'Two university experts today debunk most of the coal industry policy advocated by the Yorkshire miners' leader, Mr Arthur Scargill.

'They claim his views will lead to massive losses of jobs and markets by the end of the century.'   *Yorkshire Post*

Hobart Paper 61
Government and Enterprise
An analysis of the economics of governmental regulation or control of industry
Ivy Papps   1975   £1·00

'. . . Ivy Papps cuts vigorously through the tangle of thinking which has surrounded the objectives and procedures of state-owned industry.'   *Director*

'For students looking for a concise and reasonable account of the rationale of government intervention in industry this essay will prove extremely useful.'   M. A. King—*Economic Journal*

Background Memorandum 1

Comparative Returns from Investment in Nationalised Industries
George Polanyi 1968 £1·00

'It is not always appreciated how far Britain's nationalised sector —a very large one by international standards—is responsible for the slow economic progress of this country. [This] recent study makes it startlingly plain what a drag the State concerns really are. The author . . . has produced for the Institute of Economic Affairs a thorough investigation of the investment and returns of the different sectors of industry which ought to be compulsory reading for every important politician.'

Yorkshire Post, in an Editorial

'Mr Polanyi estimates that if the entire public sector had matched the rate of return of the private sector, the additional annual growth of output would have been 1·2 per cent.' *Guardian*

Background Memorandum 2

Contrasts in Nationalised Transport Since 1947
George Polanyi 1968 £1·00

'This memorandum singles out the record of nationalised transport during 20 years in which the tug-of-war between commercial and social (and political) criteria has pulled railway management first one way and then another.' *Board of Trade Review*

'. . . this second memorandum . . . is concentrated upon the British Railways Board and the Transport Holding Company. Financial results for both organisations are stated in very summary form and not analysed in any extended way. The financial performance of the railways is ascribed to the failure of successive governments to give clear guidance on whether social or commercial objectives were to be pursued. In slightly more precise terms the policy of the railways is found to be at fault in terms of underpricing, "below cost or less than the commercially obtainable profit"; and because of undue reliance upon "investment in modernisation".' *Economic Journal*

Background Memorandum 3

The Postal Service: Competition or Monopoly?
Ian Senior 1970 50p

'. . . proposes an end to the Post Office's statutory monopoly of letter carrying, the charging of economic prices for this service (i.e. higher charges for deliveries in rural areas, unless explicitly subsidised), and greater independence for local post office managers in setting commercial policy.

'These suggestions are quite consistent with much current thinking about the nationalised industries. They should also appeal to those who—rightly—advocate devolution, geographical and managerial, as one remedy to the growing bureaucracy of central government.' *New Society*

HOBART PAPERS in print